Abbott and Ellwood
Hallelujah (detail) 2010

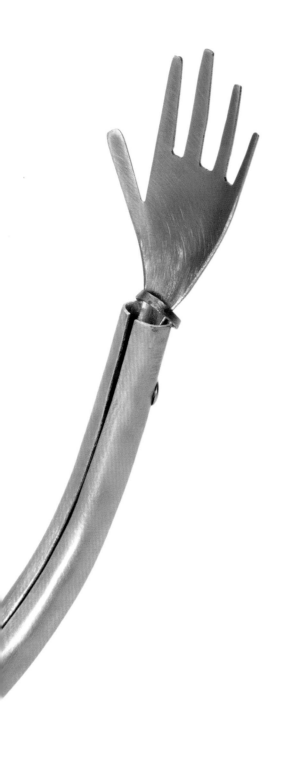

Smile

Foreword

Smile comprises works by thirteen leading contemporary applied artists linked by the theme of one of the simplest but most emotive words in our language – 'Smile'.

Curated by Mary La Trobe-Bateman, 'Smile' looks at how makers have explored the quintessentially British love of everyday humour. Many of the works suggest memories of childhood and long-ago holidays or explore the comedy in ordinary life. Eleanor Glover's five letters spelling out the word smile are like characters at a party. Craig Mitchell's illustrative ceramics include a couple valiantly trying to continue their outdoor life despite the advent of children, nappies and sleep deprivation. Lindsay Mann has created brooches she describes as 'apparatus for the promotion of cheeriness' including one that blows bubbles and transforms tin figures into curious wheeled vehicles.

The works in *Smile* are in a wide variety of genres and materials. Abbott and Ellwood exhibit humorous sculptures of people made from metal sheet printed with colourful patterns. A stop-frame glove puppet animation by Jo Lawrence depicts the strange delights that a glove maker discovers on a nocturnal journey. Textiles are strongly represented. Janet Bolton's hand-sewn Lowry-esque images, Julie Arkell's fabric and papier-mâché 'rabbit people' and Freddie Robins' balls of wool turned into caricatures of the sheep that produced them. Linda Miller has created 'silkie smiles' – a series of faux naive machine embroideries depicting seaside scenes – especially for this exhibition. Lucy Casson's humorous recycled metal creatures struggle with the trials of cooking on an old kitchen table and Deirdre Nelson's animal-based stitched and knitted works stem from her artist's residency on the Hebridean Isle of North Uist off the Scottish west coast.

But a smile is not always simply a sign of amusement. It can convey a host of complex emotions: be whimsical or pensive, sad or ironic. For example, the figures in Robert Race's driftwood and found materials automata appear like apprehensive reluctant heroes while Michael Flynn's ceramics dwell on the narrow line between laughter and tears. Every piece in the exhibition invites you to spend time with it – whether to uncover a deeper message or admire the maker's skills and find another aspect of the work that makes you smile and feel brighter.

A personal selection by Mary La Trobe-Bateman the exhibitors presented here span a range of media, and personal creative practices; together they illustrate the rich creative practice that exists in the UK. Deep felt thanks are due to Mary, Hephzibah Anderson, Lisa Rostron, Dewi Tannatt Lloyd and all of the exhibitors. Let us rightly celebrate and smile!

Philip Hughes, Director, Ruthin Craft Centre

Lucy Casson
Ruler 2010

Smile

Smile – the very word can be enough to light up all but the most serious countenance. Understood across time and place, it's a universal expression mastered in the cradle, long before we acquire language.

Yet despite being wordless, a smile says plenty. It transmits a message of welcome, reassurance or inclusivity. It conveys pleasure and pride, sympathy and satisfaction. The instantaneous flexing of the facial muscles at both corners of the mouth, the gentle crinkling around the eyes, a flash of pearly whites perhaps – such a simple, instinctive act, it betokens gratitude, signals understanding and can even whisper 'I love you'.

But just as a smile sweetens, so it sometimes complicates. Whereas you might be beaming joyously, another's grin could be ironic. A smile has the potential to be superior and sneering as well as kindly. And however much we're able to convey with a smile, we may use it to conceal in equal measure. When Herman Melville wrote that 'A smile is the chosen vehicle of all ambiguities,' he was merely verbalising what Da Vinci legendarily depicted in his Mona Lisa centuries earlier.

From the Big Bad Wolf's toothy leer to the grinning croc in Peter Pan, fiction and fables are full of cautionary tales that tell us beware the smiling stranger. And yet, how irresistible it remains. As human beings, we can't help but be drawn to those who offer smiles. Free to bestow, riches to receive, they ease our passage through life. Catch one on a gloomy morning, and you'll feel like a convert to Hallmark platitudes for the rest of the day.

As the title for this exhibition, 'Smile' both encapsulates the work itself and anticipates the viewer's response. Like a smile on the face of another, the collected pieces are instantly appealing. Beckoning the eye with ready charm, they radiate a simple sunniness that mimics a smile's accessibility.

On first glance, many of these exhibits exert an almost childlike pull. Some works appear to be actual toys, capable of being tugged along or spun around like Robert Race's mechanical marvels; others are merely toy-sized. It's a landscape in which the imagination runs wild, transforming an inanimate object like a glove, for instance, into a small being with a big character, as occurs in Jo Lawrence's film. Elsewhere, quasi-mechanical figures spring from Abbott and Ellwood's jewellery, crafted large-scale using techniques perfected for gem-like brooches. Anything is possible.

The 13 represented makers work in wood, metal, ceramics and textiles, but there is one medium common to all: narrative. A smile is as often a beginning as it is an end, and these innocent-seeming exhibits amply repay closer attention. Some of the stories they draw on seem to lure us back to the nursery, to tales that start 'Once upon a time' and are peopled by Lilliputians and shape changers. Stories are told in tin and timber, ornamented with ephemera and found materials. They are stitched with needle and thread or woven, quite literally, from balls of wool.

Julie Arkell
Welsh Lamb 2010

Mythological characters spring from clay with contemporary alacrity in Michael Flynn's work, while Craig Mitchell works adds metal to the mix to conjure up characters of comic-book dash. Mitchell's heroes and villains are ensnared in witty scenarios, reminding us that smiles can be secretive, too. You'll need to pause before these works to catch the sly humour of their punster titles and fully appreciate the meticulously constructed visual jokes that they enact.

Beyond their surface appeal, these works are as nuanced as any smile. Linger awhile before them, and their sunny hues and jaunty narratives yield riddling rewards and mirthful ambiguities that will make you want to return to their presence again and again. Like the fairytales whose narratives are alluded to here and there, that childishness conceals tangled, decidedly adult truths.

Julie Arkell's 'rabbit people' are instantly charming, yet what lies beneath their winsomeness? Or take Lucy Casson's miniature figures: so beguiling in their industriousness but what are they really up to? And what of Deirdre Nelson's dolled up china animals? Such questions and their imagined answers will only broaden the viewer's smile.

Just as we each smile differently, so no two pieces in this exhibition will trigger an identical response in any one person, nor will any two people experience the same reaction to any one work. Janet Bolton's fabric pictures, for example, collaged from a library of scraps that it's taken her a lifetime to build, will prompt a smile of nostalgia in some and tickled admiration in others. Similarly with Linda Miller's sewn portraits: there's a smile to be had from the subject matter – images redolent of seaside holidays and a nostalgia for simpler times – and another from the quirky juxtaposition between their homeliness and the grandiosity of the exquisite embroidery in which they're rendered. It's no wonder the people in these pieces are themselves always smiling.

Superficially, the smile is a simple response, a timeless language that pays little heed to national borders or local custom. It humanises us and transcends language. And though intensely personal, a smile also links its bearer to their antecedents. Along with the less capricious physical facts of a face – nose, ears and so on – an infant's smile can belong to a great-aunt or an aged grandpa, summoning up their memory in those who knew them.

All of this finds an echo in the folk craft traditions that so many of the assembled makers draw upon. The techniques that they have perfected and made their own were bred from necessity. Their roots are in ancient skills, scored deeply into our cultural heritage and born of utilitarian need.

Intrigue, wonder or surprise? Enchantment or a wry sense of shared mischief? Whatever the nature of your response as you explore this show, you're sure to find yourself connecting with a smile to the work, to fellow viewers, and perhaps even to a more carefree, impish version yourself.

Hephzibah Anderson

Freddie Robins
Comfort Sheep 2010

Linger, ponder & reflect

The pieces in this exhibition invite a response – perhaps a smile of surprise, perhaps a wry acknowledgement of something vaguely familiar, a childhood memory brought to the surface. First impressions soon give way to deeper sorts of enjoyment as enigmatic messages reveal themselves and hidden meanings come into focus. Whilst the work is on show to be looked at and admired, it is also here to be savoured so that the individual skills of the makers and their passionate commitment to their particular craft will work its magic on the viewer, and then you'll SMILE

I have long been fascinated by Julie Arkell's work whose immediate appeal belies the intensity and depth of the world she creates. Here, with her 'rabbit people', she has created cameo portraits – literally scenes, where the characters are involved in a photographic session and invited to 'smile' for the camera. For Julie it's the mistakes and flaws that creep into her creatures and the events that she describes in these scenarios, that appeal, and produce the humanity with which we can all identify. Lucy Casson has also created a world utterly and uniquely her own. She makes creatures out of scraps of old tins and discarded materials gathered from the streets around her south London studio and here sets them in mundane domestic situations. Through her deft manipulation of scale, a sharp and affectionate eye for the foibles of human nature, and an uncanny ability to incorporate an element of surprise, these mini installations are filled with allegory, mystery, and drama out of all proportion to their size.

Both Robert Race and Eleanor Glover make work rooted in the traditions of folk craft but the work has developed to become personal and unique. Robert is fascinated by the mechanics of the way his toys work. His moving structures are simple and ingenious and often refer to the unsophisticated pieces he has found and admired on his travels. Eleanor's work comes from a different journey – sometimes growing out of found objects but always confronting an inner emotional story linked to myths and the imaginings of the mind.

Janet Bolton's technique is a distillation of a lifetime spent using appliqué. Her collaged pictures and boxed scenes are made with a quiet simplicity: pieces of fabric are cut, placed and hand stitched together before attaching buttons, sticks or tiny objects, boxes are carefully filled. Linda Miller whose machine-embroidered pictures illustrate scenes from every day life also works with a confidence built through many years of refining her technique: here she indulges in portraying her favourite medium – water – stitching scenes of the sea and swimming that evoke the smell of the fresh salt air and the cries of gulls. At first glance the work of both these artists conjure up nostalgic memories of childhood using the sort of imagery associated with children's drawings: simplified forms in a naïve landscape. Look a little closer, though, and you see that something more complex and sophisticated is in play.

Michael Flynn and Craig Mitchell are two very different ceramicists yet both tell stories with the figures they build. Flynn has an international reputation for his porcelain figures that follow a tradition of the fine figurines that illustrate myths. However his groups are contemporary and his making has an immediacy that adds to the vitality of the figures. Although these are sometimes mere suggestions of form, the humour of their situation is clear. Mitchell's figures also describe humorous situations or illustrate puns; they derive from the comic strip characters that have always fascinated him and are built with great skill, confidently combining metal and clay to produce figures that act with panache and gusto to amuse and entertain us.

Abbott and Ellwood are known for their jewellery – charming enamelled steel brooches often of cut-out figures, animals and birds. A few years ago they started making larger scenes using the same meticulous fine jewellery techniques. Their engaging figures are almost mechanical, decorated with screen-printed patterns like those on the jewellery. Another jeweller Lindsey Mann plays with metal and small found mechanical objects, echoing the interests of her father and grandfather. For this exhibition she has made unusual, intricate and quirky tools to wear. Each tells a story and each is designed to bring comfort to the wearer and amusement in a tricky social situation.

Jo Lawrence recently spent time as artist in residence at the Victoria & Albert exploring the museum for ideas. Prompted by two particular objects in the Collection she produced the film *Glover* where animated glove creatures inhabit the edges of the world that Glover, the film's hero and glove-maker, explores. Lawrence's technique of using printed face photographs to produce each character of her imagination brings a strangeness to these sinister creatures. In the film they are brilliantly brought to life as the hands inside them behave like shadow puppeteers causing a smile of unease.

Ironic amusement is an emotion that greets the work of both Freddie Robins and Deirdre Nelson. Robin's textile practice is based on knit and here she has played with balls of wool to produce *Comfort Sheep*. Each of the seven different breeds of sheep that produce the wool is caught in the depiction of the characters of these creatures. When they are lined up on a shelf the sheep appear to be jostling for position in the flock. Nelson has also chosen found objects in order to question and reflect on our experience of textile art. Each tiny embellished china animal relates to a specific story and Nelson uses traditional stitch and knit techniques with carefully chosen materials to draw out the humour of the myth or legend.

This group of artists have made their own individual and often idiosyncratic interpretation of SMILE in the materials of their craft: an eclectic mix that includes clay, paper, wool, metal, wood, reclaimed materials and recycled objects. They share a lightness of touch as well as a serious pursuit of ideas. Linger, ponder and reflect then break into a smile.

Mary La Trobe-Bateman

Eleanor Glover
Smile (detail) 2010

Abbott and Ellwood

In the studio we are surrounded by imagery which we reference almost by osmosis, connecting our thoughts through sketching and drawing and a constant dialogue with each other. Working with an intuitive response to our collection of printed metal and found objects, we proceed symbiotically, not quite knowing where the journey will lead.

With the figure as a framework, we set off with our thoughts to find the story that each piece has to tell, taking on a life of their own through the making, perhaps expressing optimism or expectancy, a joie de vivre that reflects our hopes and dreams… tinged with humour or maybe pathos. An eclectic and very personal collection emerges, which we hope makes a connection with the viewer and, perhaps, brings a smile!

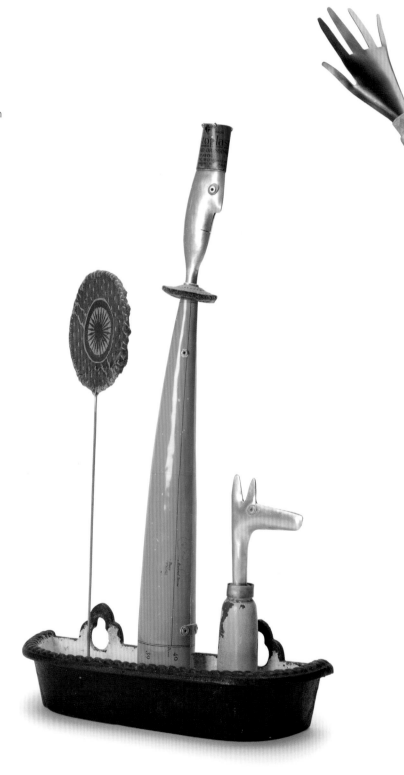

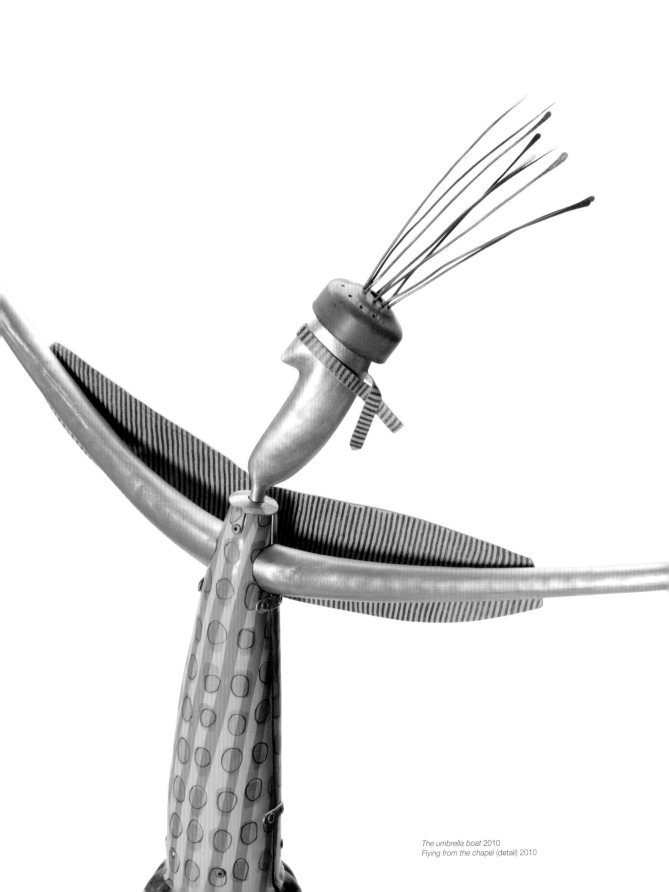

The umbrella boat 2010
Flying from the chapel (detail) 2010

Julie Arkell

Someone says 'smile' and I hear the click of a camera. A photograph is taken, a memory made. 'Smile' is often a command and a hope for a good picture. When I look at photographs I see moments captured over the years.

Preparing for this exhibition I remembered a small pocket album I found in my aunt's house. The photo frames were cut out with scissors, and the pages joined together with red and white stripey perforated paper. A few faces were familiar to me, but many others looked unknown and curious. This inspired me to make my own 'pocket album', filling it with a make believe family in their own hand cut frames of sugar paper. It seems to me there is a mystery in photographs, a story we will never fully know, fragments captured when a smile is demanded.

The day I nearly lost poor lamby 2010

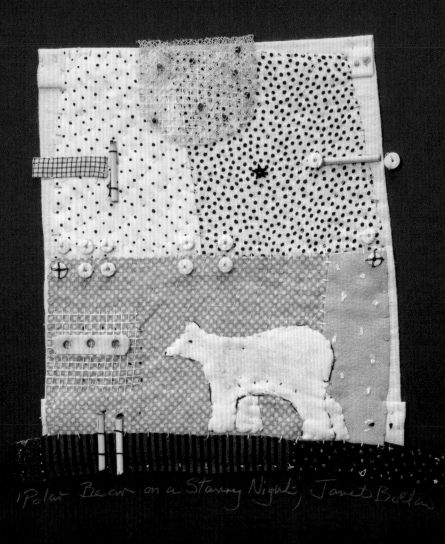

'Polar Bear on a Starry Night', Janet Bolton

Janet Bolton

Found objects, for example driftwood and buttons, have for many years been an integral part of my work. Last year, small objects that I had previously used as subject matter became the work themselves, components of three dimensional pieces. Before this I would sometimes make an object in response to a fabric piece and exhibit them together. Now the object itself has become the subject matter from which I build a fabric piece.

This making of a three dimensional piece and then using it as subject matter is a new departure. Maybe one that I will continue for many years, maybe not, who knows.

The Polar Bear 2010
Polar Bear Box 2010

Lucy Casson

Working with tin, cloth and found objects
I am recently also using inks, mark making
and finger printing. My aim is to achieve
spontaneity, combining the immediacy
of drawing with the time-consuming
processes of making.

Man and dog 2010

Michael Flynn

There is a precipice between laughter and tears. A joke can trip nimbly along that knife-edge relying upon a comprehension which may fail, may plunge it into the tenebrae of misunderstanding. The rictus of a smile poised at that moment of decision: to smirk, to guffaw, to titter, to frown, to sneer, to turn away or simply not to want to understand. A burgeoning smile might be the first indication of precariousness. Balanced on a needle tip between what has been and what might be, between the banal and the ludicrous, life performed before us, around us, a dramaturgy from which we cannot escape.

To draw together disparate elements. To play with form and surface, idea and observation. A linear dynamic offset by a delicacy of colouration, of tonality. Perhaps to get closer to that point which is the rudiment of a smile.

Entourage 2010

Eleanor Glover

This eclectic set of letters may resemble five flamboyant characters at a loud party. They do not interact with each other, and evidently speak different languages but each contributes to a whole which has a celebratory feel.

I also wanted to reflect the crazy surrealism and breaking of rules which lie beneath so much which makes one lucky enough to break into a smile.

Shadow Theatre in a Suitcase 2010
Smile (detail) 2010

Glover 2010

Jo Lawrence

The work here consists of 'Glover', a stopframe animation and includes some of the original glove puppets animated in the Gloveland carnival scenes with additional glove creatures developed subsequently. It's impossible to view the hollow puppet glove without also seeing it's latent potential for performance, signalled by the possibility that a hand could suddenly occupy the glove and bring it to life.

Glover tells the story of the journey of a glovemaker. The film integrates a masked actor as a 'human puppet' and animated gloves. The arrival of a mysterious colourful map prompts a strange journey to the edge of the world, transforming Glover's monochromatic existence. Glover's journey takes him to the furthest reaches of his imagination, Terra Chirotheca, Gloveland, a place of both horror and delight, where he meets a series of strange hybrids – part beast or human, part glove.

MODEL NO. 4868
INSTRUCTIONS FOR USE:
USE EMERGENCY BUBBLE-BLOWING
KIT TO CALM OPPOSING PARTIES IN
THE EVENT OF AN ALTERCATION.

Lindsey Mann

From childhood I have had a fascination
for old tools, the older they are and
more mysterious the better. Not really
understanding what a tool is for, provides
the perfect opportunity for a little imagination
to come into play and a story to unravel.

Taking inspiration from bizarre Victorian
inventions and the Heath-Robinson
approach to fabrication I have created my
own series of tools for coping with everyday
scenarios and to help turn an awkward social
situation on its head. The idea of spreading
a little joy and happiness rather appeals, so
drawing inspiration from these ideas I have
created a series of wearable tools which will
undoubtedly aid the wearer and help them
to spread a little cheeriness too. Just as a
clown hides behind a painted smile, these
tools might provide a comic shield for the
ill at ease.

Emergency bubble-blowing kit –
brooch with display stand 2010
Extractor fan – brooch with
display stand 2010

Linda Miller

Using my distinctive, unique style I create
rich, colourful, naïve and humorous machine
embroideries which contain figures set in
the out-doors, always smiling and usually
depicted within a story. I grew up sewing
and living by the sea, and those are two of
the things I love the best. I swim regularly
and love being under the water, propelling
myself along and being surrounded by the
watery colour blue.

All the people in my work smile because
mostly my people are genuinely happy
and contented and busy being about their
business. This expression of happiness can
occasionally be deceptive to the viewer, a
lull into a false sense of security within the
subject matter of the piece. A character can
easily convey this happy appearance which
is not really as honest as it first seems.

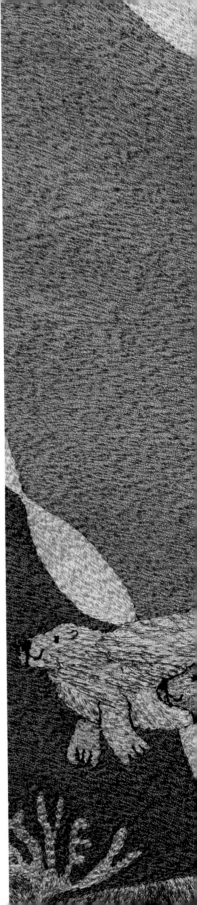

Silkie Smiles 2010

Craig Mitchell

My work explores contemporary culture and universal themes but it is also a response to current events, usually personal. Chance comments, memories and interesting lines or words often act as triggers for ideas, which I like to realise in a humorous way. I use various devices to achieve this including exaggerated movements or proportions, unlikely scenarios or ridiculous juxtapositions. At a deeper level I am hinting at self destructive urges in difficult times which I interpret in a humorous way to sugar the pill.

I am also fascinated by the dichotomy of marrying something as transitory as a joke with such a permanent material as clay. This poses questions: can humour remain relevant over time? be universal? cross cultural? And leads to the editing and paring down of my ideas to their essence.

Elephant 2008
Dowry 2008

Deirdre Nelson

The work is a development of pieces I produced in North Uist on an artists residency where I gathered local stories relating to past and present and created a series of animal-based works. These include the story of an elephant washed up on a Hebridean shore, a cow having the same value as a spinning wheel in a dowry, sheep having gold teeth due to the gold dust in the land, alongside contemporary interpretations of a deer with glow in the dark cover (who appears on dark roads unannounced).

Each piece relates to a specific animal story and uses traditional stitch and knit techniques to take a humorous look at them. Materials such as silk, wool, gold leaf and merino wool are carefully chosen to be relevant to each story.

Robert Race

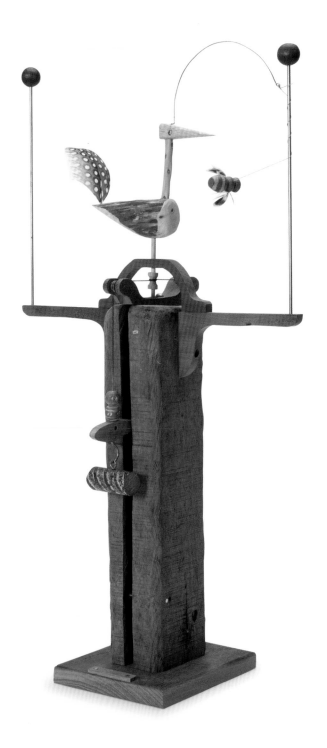

I like working with driftwood because it always carries a good back-story. It was part of a living tree; it was new timber, possibly transported for thousands of miles, or merely a fruit box or a scrubbing brush. All this leaves its marks; the colours of rust staining, eroded paint layers and bleaching by sun and salt; the polished smoothness, and the strange textures, produced by natural sandblasting or by the activities of crustaceans and molluscs.

In my work I try to combine these ambiguous echoes of former lives with playful representations; and to bring those representations to life through movement. The challenge is to use simple mechanisms, in full view, and still achieve a suspension of disbelief. My protagonists often appear slightly apprehensive. They hesitate. They seem unheroic, but they persist, as heroes might.

Bird and Bee 2010

Freddie Robins

My 'Comfort Creatures' are an embodiment of the emotional attachment that I have to wool. I love wool. Through adulthood I have amassed a large amount of odd balls and balls of wool. I have bought wool all over the world from Bangladesh to Berlin, South Africa to Shetland. These odd balls are of no use to me. I can't, and don't want to, make anything from them, but I am compelled to buy them.

My 'Comfort Creatures' are a personification of this useless wool, an attempt to turn my feelings towards an undervalued, everyday material into tangible objects that it is socially acceptable to love. In this particular series of 'Comfort Sheep' I have turned the ball of wool into a caricature of the sheep breed that the wool originally came from – Jacob, Blue Faced Leicester, Grey Cheviot, Black Welsh, Wensleydale, Swaledale and Dalesbred.

Comfort Sheep 2010

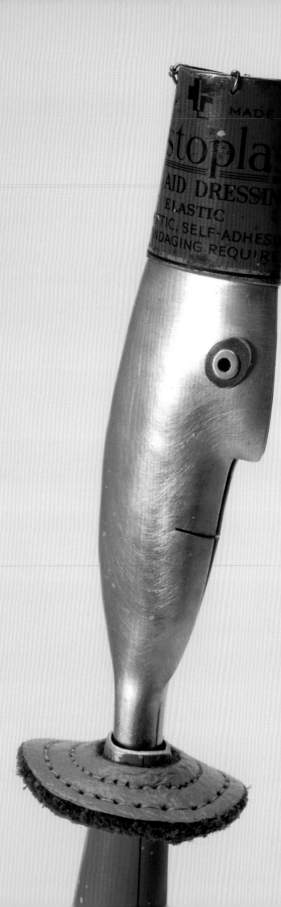

Mary La Trobe-Bateman would like to thank all the makers
for their enthusiasm and the work made especially for this
exhibition, Philip Hughes, Hephzibah Anderson, Jane Gerrard
and Lisa Rostron at Lawn.

Ruthin Craft Centre would like to thank Mary La Trobe-Bateman,
Hephzibah Anderson and all of the exhibited artists;
Greg Parsons; Lisa Rostron, Stephen Heaton and
Aled Morris Brown at Lawn; Dewi Tannatt Lloyd; Hafina Clwyd;
Pete Goodridge and ArtWorks and the Arts Council of Wales.

The publishers would like to thank the Arts Council of Wales.
RCC thank The Esmée Fairbairn Foundation for their support.

Curated by Mary La Trobe-Bateman; Exhibition organisation:
Philip Hughes; Design: Lisa Rostron at Lawn; Photography:
Dewi Tannatt Lloyd (except Deirdre Nelson); Logistics:
Pete Goodridge and ArtWorks; Translations: Hafina Clwyd.
RCC staff: Philip Hughes, Jane Gerrard, Elen Bonner,
Einir Wyn Jones, Olga Byrne, Sue Edwards and
Roger Mansbridge. A Welsh Language version is available.

Published by Ruthin Craft Centre.
Text © The Authors 2010. ISBN 978-1-905865-26-0
Ruthin Craft Centre, The Centre for the Applied Arts, Park Road,
Ruthin, Denbighshire LL15 1BB Tel: +44 (0)1824 704774
www.ruthincraftcentre.org.uk

Ruthin Craft Centre is part of Denbighshire County Council and
is revenue funded by the Arts Council of Wales.

Smile is a RCC Touring Exhibition.

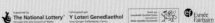

Abbott and Ellwood
The umbrella boat (detail) 2010